Depressed?
What does the Bible say about Depression?.

By: Susan D. Smith

Depressed?
What does the Bible say about Depression?

By Susan D. Smith

ISBN-13: 978-1505972528
ISBN-10:1505972523

Cover Design by Susan D. Smith

Printed in the United States of America.

This book may be purchased online at:
http://amazon.com
and other fine book sellers.

Bookstores and churches, etc., may purchase this book at wholesale for resale or distribution.

DEDICATION

This book is dedicated to first of all, to my God, the Lord Jesus, who is leading me each and every step of the way.

Then it is dedicated to my husband who passed away August 25, 2013 who encouraged me to follow God and was my staunchest supporter. I can still hear him saying, Go for it, Susie. You've got to obey God.

Then it's dedicated to my children Joseph Smith and Leah Simpson with her husband Evan. I love all three of you and am so proud of the successful adults you have become! A special thank you to my mother who taught me to believe in impossibilities becoming possibilities.

Lastly this book is dedicated to the people God has blessed me with in my life. Many may never know their true impact on my life but God does and after all, that's all that really matters

My father, Joseph M. Wine who passed away April 7, 2014

Bishop James Kilgore who passed away February 5, 2014

Bishop & Sis. Tommy Craft

Bro. & Sis. Ron Macey

Bro. & Sis. Howard Watson

Bro. John & Sis. Aurelia Hopkins

Bro. & Sister Doug Joseph

Bro. & Sis. E.S. Harper

Sister Beverly Haygood

Sister Regina Horne

Bro. & Sis. T. L. Dobbs

Sis. Theresa Neal of Theresa Marie Photography & Design for my bio pictures. There are many more but these are the ones that stand out to me. Please know that I love everyone who has impacted my life and I could never thank you enough.

Colossians 1:11

11 Strengthened with all might, according to his glorious power, unto all patience and longsuffering with joyfulness;

1 Peter 4:12

12 Beloved, think it not strange concerning the fiery trial which is to try you, as though some strange thing happened unto you:

Foreword

I feel this is an area that is rarely covered in our movement and because it is not, many suffer under misconceptions. The Jews believed strongly that "when you do good, good things happen to you", but we know that is not really the way it is. The disciples asked the Lord "who did sin.."(the man born blind) because they felt some sin has to happen for bad things to come into a life...we know that is not true. Bad things happen to good people, but what do they do when it happens? You are addressing these issues and I think it is great. Instead of "why me" we should be asking "what does this mean".

Bro. Ron Macey, Pastor
Royalwood, Houston, Texas

A note from the Author

I was always the one who saw the glass as half full, not half empty with a ready smile. Now the smile is still in place but I have a lot of days where it doesn't quite reach my eyes because my heart is shredded but I'm getting better. You see, the secret is time on my knees, my face buried in the carpet getting close to the King of Kings and the Lord of Lords. That's where I find peace and where you can find peace.

Even going from a table for five to a table for one you can find happiness just you and Jesus. So for now and probably the rest of my days on earth it will just be me and Jesus. So when I worship Jesus and it is extreme you must realize the relationship Jesus and I have

I have nothing left to lose. I've already lost it.

When you see someone worshipping God with abandon realize there has been a great price paid for worship like that. When you hear a great preacher or see a saint pray with great anointing know that only came by going through the fire!

This book was developed from deep dark days after my husband's death and on the heels of that Bishop James Kilgore's death and then my father's death. The Bishop had been on speed dial for me for many years while I was battling cancer. During that battle I didn't have time to be depressed much because there were teenagers in the house.

When my husband passed away I not only lost my soul mate but I lost my best friend, then my family, and lastly the Bishop. If it had not been for Bishop T. L. & Sister Diann Craft, along with friends who stepped up to check on me on that lonely Thanksgiving, Christmas, Valentine's day I probably would not be here. Yes, I got that depressed.

Even Christians can contemplate suicide. It's not in thinking about it but it's in doing it because once it's done it can't be undone. As long as you're breathing you can repent.

All of us go through things. Whatever you are going through to you is a crisis and can cause severe depression and despondency. This is how God talked to me during that time. I hope and pray somehow this helps you.

Realize this was day by day. You can choose to read it as a daily devotional or all at once. It's up to you but I think it should be taken daily like medicine to help you understand what you may be going through.

Know that I love you and pray for those I have never met every day who are battling depression and despondency because of the fire they may be walking through. We have to realize God never said we would live a life of roses because of living for him but that there would be trials, fiery trials.

When God was giving me these individual thoughts I felt like the sun was setting on my life. I felt like it was over. God, however, has bigger plans. We have to realize that putting our life in God's hands and in truly giving Him all we will find joy like we never thought possible.

As one of my friends says, Keep pressin'! (Sissy Hudson)

Contents

Questioning God

Do you think you are the only one who has ever questioned God? Really?

Look at King David:

Psalm 10:1

10 "Why standest thou afar off, O Lord? why hidest thou thyself in times of trouble?"

Psalms 77

1 I cried unto God with my voice, even unto God with my voice; and he gave ear unto me. 2 In the day of my trouble I sought the Lord: my sore ran in the night, and ceased not: my soul refused to be comforted.3 I remembered God, and was troubled: I complained, and my spirit was overwhelmed. Selah. 4 Thou holdest mine eyes waking: I am so troubled that I cannot speak. 5 I have considered the days of old, the years of ancient times. 6 I call to remembrance my song in the night: I commune with mine own heart: and my spirit made diligent search. 7 Will the Lord cast off for ever? and will he be favourable no more?8 Is his mercy clean gone for ever? doth his promise fail for evermore? 9 Hath God forgotten to be gracious? hath he in anger shut up his tender mercies? Selah. 10 And I said, This is my infirmity: but I will remember the years of the right hand of the most High. 11 I will remember the works of the LORD: surely I will remember thy wonders of old. 12 I will meditate also of all thy work, and talk of thy doings. 13 Thy way, O God, is in the sanctuary: who is so great a God as our God? 14 Thou art the God that doest wonders: thou hast declared thy strength among the people. 15 Thou hast with thine arm redeemed thy people, the sons of Jacob and Joseph. Selah. 16 The waters saw thee, O God, the waters saw thee; they were afraid: the depths also were troubled. 17 The clouds poured out water: the skies sent out a sound: thine arrows also went abroad. 18 The voice of thy thunder was in the heaven: the lightnings lightened the world: the earth trembled

*and shook. [19] Thy way is in the sea, and thy path in the great
waters, and thy footsteps are not known. [20] Thou leddest thy
people like a flock by the hand of Moses and Aaron.*

During the writing of this book I questioned God a lot. I didn't
understand why these things had to happen to me. No, I did not
have a get out of jail free card because I'm a Christian. Many
times during the writing of this book I remember feeling like
David in Psalms 6:6,

Psalm 6:6

*[6] I am weary with my groaning; all the night make I my bed to
swim; I water my couch with my tears.*

I would be weeping and not even know it until I realized I was
wet. That is depression.

This book talks mainly about overcoming but in order for me to
walk through the depression God taught me about being an
overcomer.

Humiliation versus Humbleness

Humiliation

Yesterday God started talking to me about these two words. They come from the same root word. In one way their meanings are completely different yet in another way very similar. I know I'm speaking in circles so read what I've written and think about it.

Define Humiliation

Someone feels ashamed and foolish because their dignity or self-respect has been injured.

Now let's look at the Bible and see what it has to say. We'll start in Acts 8:32-33 where it talks of Jesus being humiliated.

"The place of the Scripture which he read was this, He was led as a sheep to the slaughter; and like a lamb dumb before his shearer, so opened he not his mouth: In his humiliation his judgment was taken away: and who shall declare his generation? For his life is taken from the earth."

Jesus suffered humiliation for us. When we start to suffer persecution for what we believe and we feel humiliated we are identifying with Him in another way. It's not in what happens to us, it's in how we handle what happens to us.

We may think we have been humiliated. Consider what Jesus went through. We struggle with persecution but we must get stronger because as wickedness prevails the persecution will also become more prominent.

Nobody wants to talk about this but it is coming. It is as much a part of the last days as the great revival. In times past when great revival was poured out great persecution and troubled times were also in abundance.

As Americans, we are all so blessed with our abundance. We are soft. James 1:10 speaks of humility in a different way. How will we react when we have nothing but God?

James 1:10 says, "But the rich, in that he is made low: because as the flower of the grass he shall pass away."

HUMILITY BEFORE THE LORD

Lastly, on humility I want to go back to Ezra 9:5. The word humiliate is not in this passage but its meaning is clear.

When we really humiliate (we become truly ashamed for our sin, the sins of our country) ourselves before the Lord is when we grow the most spiritually. Humiliation of this type is healthy spiritually. Ezra shows us how.

Ezra 9:5-6

"And at the evening sacrifice I arose up from my heaviness; and having rent my garments and my mantle, I fell upon my knees, and spread out my hands unto the Lord my God, And said, O my God, I am ashamed and blush to lift up my face to thee, my God: for our iniquities are increased over our head and our trespass is grown up into the heavens."

What God is talking to me about here is the sin of our generation, our country. You can legalize drugs. You can say it is okay for people to live together before marriage. We can ignore gossip and backbiting as normal today. People can even say homosexuality is not a sin. But we will still put people in prison for murder and the Bible is very plain that all of these are sin.

Why did I go there?

Because it's time, it's time we get serious about our walk with God. We have to fall on our faces in embarrassment for the sins

that have become acceptable in our country and our generation.

When we want revival, really want revival, we won't argue with people. That is when we will go to our knees. We will go door knocking.We will travail before God because of our sin and theirs. The way we have acted towards them is also sin but no one wants to mention that.

We can hate the sin but we must love the sinner.

How do you treat people who are different from you?

Would Jesus be ashamed of you?

Tomorrow I will share what God has been talking to me about humbleness and then how the two are similar yet dissimilar.

Each milestone since my love's death brings a wave of fresh pain but I'm finding I rest easier as each month passes in the comforting arms of Jesus. Five months ago today my world rocked precariously but my God reached His hand out to me and calmed me in the midst of the rocking.

That's the God we serve. He's with us on the mountaintop and even more so in the turbulence of the valley.

Humbleness

We say we want to be humble before God but do we really understand its full meaning? This morning I'm focused on humbleness, yesterday it was humiliation. Let's see where this takes us.

Define humble

Having or showing a modest or low estimate of one's own importance.

Now let's see what the Bible has to say about being humble.

Proverbs 29:23 says, *"A man's pride shall bring him low: but honour shall uphold the humble in spirit."*

Matthew 23:12 *"And whosoever shall exalt himself shall be abased; and he that shall humble himself shall be exalted."*

John 3:30. *"He must increase, but I must decrease."*

Micah 6:8, *"He have shewed thee, O man, what is good; and what doth the Lord require of thee, but to do justly, and to love mercy, and to walk humbly with God."*

There are so many passages in the Bible on being humble. Being humble does not mean you allow others to walk all over you. All it means is that you're not proud.

We have to work at this. It is a daily thing. As humans we are naturally proud of our families, proud of what we've accomplished, proud of who we are but we cannot allow pride to come between us and God. We must be humble.

We must realize that everything God has blessed us with and allowed us to accomplish has come from God. When we realize that and we give God the glory for all He has done that's when

our relationship with Him changes. When somebody applauds you for what you've done you need to turn that applause to God.

Now that I'm traveling, writing books and evangelizing sometimes people like to say great things about me. Bishop Kilgore taught me by example that when they do that you must turn it back to praise to Jesus. After things like that you have to take yourself off by yourself because our flesh loves to be petted and applauded with great words. The devil so wants us to get caught up in this.

When people have honored me for accomplishments that's when I have to take myself off to pray. I have to get down on all fours. I have to be as low as I can get in the presence of God. I have to make sure that I become as humble as possible and then try to be more humble.

Colossians 2:18 says it best
"Let no man beguile you of your reward in a voluntary humility and worshiping of angels, intruding into those things which he hath not seen, vainly puffed up by his fleshly mind."

If we are not careful we can become so important in our own minds that we try to put ourselves in God's place. This passage lets us know that we should not be puffed up in our own minds so it's very important that we learn how to humble ourselves or God will humble us.

WHAT IS TRUE HUMBLENESS?

Psalms 51:17 says,
"The sacrifices of God are a broken spirit a broken and a contrite heart, O God, that wilt not despise."

We should all humble ourselves in the presence of God.

Tomorrow I will show the comparison between humility and humbleness. Please understand this is how God talks to me and effects change in me. I pray it helps someone to come closer to God.

How are humility and being
humble alike?

Humbleness is when we show or feel a modest or low estimate of our own importance.

While humility and humbleness are alike they're also very different. Humility in my eyes = shame while humbleness = not prideful.

We want God to do great things among us but we have to understand the importance of humility and humbleness before him. I think to get a real grip on this we need to understand sanctification (consecration) before God.

SANCTIFICATION (CONSECRATION)

Joshua 3:5 says
"And Joshua said unto the people, Sanctify yourselves: for to morrow the Lord will do wonders among you."

- How do we sanctify ourselves?

We don't. God does. However, this is a process that we have to allow God to work on us. Humility and humbleness before God are integral to this process.

We have to remember that no matter what we think of ourselves or how righteous we may appear it only matters what God thinks. Isaiah put it in the best perspective. We say our perception is our reality.

- What about God's perception of us?

Isaiah 64:6 says, *"But we are all as an unclean thing, and all our righteousnesses are as filthy rags;..."*

--Brokenness

If we truly want to be as Jesus, it will cost us. There will not be too many who are willing to be placed on the potter's wheel. God truly wants to make and mold us after Him but we are so unwilling to be molded. No one likes pain. To be molded you must be broken. To be broken causes excruciating pain.

Jeremiah 18:4
"And the vessel that he made of clay was marred in the hand of the potter: so he made it again another vessel, as seemed good to the potter to make it."

We want it to seem good to us. It doesn't matter what we want. It only matters what God, our potter, wants. What may seem good to us may be the exact opposite to God.

SANCTIFICATION THROUGH THE WORD OF GOD

John 17:16-17
"They are not of the world, even as I am NOT of the world. Sanctify then through thy truth: thy word is truth."

--Our reasonable service

True humility and humbleness before God will take us to our knees for we will do as Romans 12 verse 1:
"I beseech you therefore, brethren, by the mercies of God, that ye present your bodies a living sacrifice, holy, acceptable unto God, which is your reasonable service."

We must remember if we walk away from everything to do the work of God we are just doing our reasonable service. It is the same as being broken on the potter's wheel. We have to realize it's all about Jesus.

Whatever talent you possess or don't possess belongs to God. If people put you on a pedestal you are responsible for giving the glory back to God. More importantly, you are responsible for humbling yourself in humility before God.

-- Deeper consecration

When we really understand this is when we will see our consecration to God deepen to a new level. Our ministries will grow. We will be led by the Spirit of God into new dimensions and greater heights. But first, we must remember how Ezra went before God.

Ezra 9:5-6
"And at the evening sacrifice I arose up from my heaviness; and having rent my garment and my mantle, I fell upon my knees, and spread out my hands unto the Lord my God. And said, O my God, I am ashamed and blush to lift up my face to thee, my God:..."

How long has it been since you or I went before God like this?

Is your spiritual thermostat in a downward spiral like America's?

With everything that is going on in our country or not going on when it comes to standing for morality I have to question whether, we as Christians, are hot or cold? Or, God forbid, have we become lukewarm?

Do we even know our own spiritual temperature and its implications?

Revelation 3:15-16
"I know thy works, that thou art neither cold nor hot: I would thou wert cold or hot. So then because thou art lukewarm, and neither cold nor hot, I will spue thee out of my mouth."

Do you know who you are spiritually?

Do you know what you stand for?

When God started talking to me about the spiritual temperature in a free fall downward I wondered where He would take me. Well, He took me also to II Peter 2:4-8 where it says,.

"For if God spared not the angels that sinned but cast them down to hell, and delivered them into chains of darkness, to be reserved unto judgement; and spared not the old world, but saved Noah the eighth person, a preacher of righteousness, bringing in the flood up on the world of the ungodly, and turning the cities of Sodom and Gomorrah into ashes condemned them with an overthrow, making them an ensample unto those that after should live ungodly; and delivered just Lot, vexed with the building conversation of the wicked: (For that righteous man dwelling among them, in seeing and hearing, vexed his righteous so from day to day with their unlawful deeds;)"

Lot chose to live next to sin. He raised his children where it touched them day in and day out. We allow things in our lives and homes that touch us and our families never realizing the price we will have to pay.

I wonder how many watched television and movies and are not offended with the display of gay marriage and witchcraft? I agree we should love the sinner but we also must take a stand against sin.

Have we become so weak in our walk with God that we do not know how to let people know that while we love them we will stand against their sin? Are we afraid of the price we may have to pay?

It's time to say, ENOUGH!

You won't be able to do that if you don't know where you stand with God. How do you know? Well, through prayer and reading His Word. It's called daily consecration. Every day start your day and end your day with God.

The question today is are you hot, cold or in that awful place of lukewarmness?

I love working for God and sharing about the miracles He has blessed me with.

I just got off the phone from another call the pancreatic cancer action network sent to me. That's three families across the U.S. I've talked to about pancreatic cancer, encouraged and shared God's love with.

That is what it's all about giving our all so people will be drawn to Jesus

For those that have watched as my world has spun out of control I have had my highs and a lot of lows. However, every morning I do my best to open my mouth and simply say, Jesus, I love you. I worship you. I thank you. I praise you. I love you, Jesus.

Well, today the emptiness of the house got to me. Yes, my husband passed away but our children.. that's all I will say about them... God knows.

I began to wonder what's the use, I'm tired, take me. I'm all alone and useless. Yes, God has blessed me and given me great miracles but I'm human and tired. Then I started studying and found I'm in good company. Many great people of God have felt this way.

So instead of letting it get the best of me I have studied and written a study on Depression, Despondency, and how to overcome it.

But today I will encourage myself in the Lord by listening to songs and reading the Bible
****

Depression and Despondency

Depression

Define Depression

Severe despondency and dejection, typically felt over a period of time and accompanied by feelings of hopelessness and inadequacy.

Depression is scattered throughout the Bible. Do not think you are alone when you feel this way. It is not what you feel but in how you handle those feelings. Take them to your God.

Elijah, David, Abraham, Peter, Jacob, Job, Jonah, Paul, Isaiah, and many others battled with depression in the Bible.

Biblical Examples

--David

Psalms 40:1-3 (I didn't and usually I don't but David did)

"I waited patiently for the Lord and He inclined unto me, and heard my cry. He brought me up also out of an horrible pit, out of the miry clay, and set my feet upon a rock, and established my goings. And He hath put a new song in my mouth even praise unto our God: many shall see it, and fear, and shall trust in the Lord."

--Moses

Numbers 11:14 (Burden of the people too heavy for him.)
" I am not able to bare all this people alone, because it is too heavy for me."

--Jonah

Seemingly depression is always worse after a great victory when

other problems seemingly happen. Jonah is one great example. This is after he came out of the whale of the fish and after Nineveh repented.

Jonah 4:3
"Therefore now, O Lord, take I beseech thee, my life from me for it is better for me to die then to live."

Yes, after having experienced all of that he became so depressed all he wanted to do was die. When depressed things don't make sense. Reasons to live evaporate. That's when you speak his name, Jesus.

--Paul

II Corinthians 7:5-6
"For when we were come in to Macedonia, our flesh had no rest, but we were troubled on every side; without were fightings, within were fears. Nevertheless God, that comforteth those that are cast down, comforted us by the coming of Titus."

GOD HEARS

I don't want to just leave you with depression today so here's one little jewel to help you if you're battling depression. Remember all you have to do is call that name. That name is Jesus. He will deliver you just like it says below:

Psalms 34:17
"The righteous cry and the Lord heareth, and delivereth them out of all their troubles."

He will deliver us!

Despondency

- Define Despondency

A state of low spirits caused by loss of hope or courage.

After studying depression, despondency seems to me the next step down. This is where we have to get a grip. We have to get a handle on us and a handle on our God. Let's look at some Biblical examples of despondency.

--Abraham

Genesis 17:15-17 says, *"And God said unto Abraham, as for Sarai thy wife, thou shalt not call her name Sarai, but Sarah shall her name be. And I will bless her, and give thee a son also of her: yea, I will bless her, and she shall be a mother of nations; kings of people shall be of her. Then Abraham fell upon his face, and laughed, and said in his heart, shall a child be born unto him that is an hundred years old? And shall Sarah that is ninety years old, bear?"*

Let's talk about despondency.

God, himself, was talking to Abraham yet he laughed and in his heart mocked the promise God gave him. You think you're the only one hopeless. Abraham was sure he had the market cornered. God gave him a promise he never expected God to fulfill.

What about you? Has God given you some promises you don't think He can fulfill? He is still God!

What made Abraham think he knew more than God? What makes you or I think that?

--Hezekiah

Isaiah 38:9-12
*"The writing of Hezekiah king of Judah, when he been sick, and
was recovered of his sickness: I said in the cutting off of my days,
I shall go to the gates of my grave: I am deprived of the residue
off my years. I said, I shall not see the Lord, even the Lord, and
the land of the living: I shall behold man no more with the
inhabitants of the world. Mine age is departed, and is removed
from me as a shepherd's tent: I have cut off like a weaver my
life: he will cut me off with pining sickness from day even tonight
wilt thou make an end of me."*

People get sick all the time. For some reason when Christians
get sick if we don't get well immediately we think God has
deserted us. What if? What if we have to go through the valley
to be what God wants us to be and to go where He wants us to
go?

--Elijah

I Kings 19:4, 9 ,
4. *"But he himself went a day's journey into the wilderness, and
came and sat down under a juniper tree: and he requested for
himself that he might die; and said, It is enough; now, O Lord,
take away my life; for I am not better than my fathers."*
9. *"And he came thither unto a cave, and lodged there; and
behold, the word of the Lord came to him, and he said unto him,
What doest thou here, Elijah?"*

I love Elijah. He is so human. After great things have happened
he goes out into the wilderness to die. This is a man that called
fire down from heaven and killed soldiers, over 50 at one time
and he did it more than once! All of a sudden he's become a
chicken.

Then if it doesn't beat all God comes to him after he continues to run and hide. Now, he's in a cave and God wants to know why?

Are you running from something that you shouldn't be afraid of? Is God hunting for you to ask you why? Is God hunting for me to ask me why?

That's really got to be hopeless. Angels touched him and fed him. Do angels not touch us and feed us when it is necessary? God had done amazing things already in his ministry yet he was scared. Put yourself in his shoes.

Why are we afraid?

--Paul

Acts 27:20
"*And when neither sun nor stars in many days appeared, and no small tempest lay on us, all hope that we should be saved was taken away.*"

Everyone, at some point, has feelings of hopelessness or despondency. That's when the scriptures we have written on our hearts should help us.

Psalms 27:1
"*The Lord is my light and my salvation; whom, shall I fear? the Lord is the strength of my life; of whom shall I be afraid?*"

How to be an Overcomer

Overcoming

Define overcoming

succeed in dealing with a problem or difficulty

Before starting I need to put a disclaimer for those that think only substandard people battle this. I've got news for you! Some of the most successful highly motivated people battle this routinely. No one is exempt.

You know I actually feel sorry for folks who have never battled this. Today this is the last thing I want to write about but it is important because they're so many people battling it. I am one of those. You really get to know Jesus by going through trials and tribulations that bring you to the point of depression and despondency.

Don't think for one minute I'm giving you an excuse to stay hopeless. I'm not! God gave this to me to give me a swift kick in the backside. So, I battled one of the, if not the most deadly form of cancer, my children backslid, my husband died of a prescription drug overdose, car problems, in law problems, insurance issues, frozen pipes and the list goes on.

BIG HOOEY!

It is nothing in God's eyes. It's time we were truly overcomers and not just for looks. You know what I mean, most of us don't have a clue what being an overcomer really is. Let's take a journey through the scriptures and see what they tell us.

Search the Scriptures
DAILY

Acts 17:11
"Those were more noble than those in Thessalonica, in that they received the word with all readiness of mind, and search the Scriptures daily, whether those things were so."

It is not good enough to just search the Scriptures but you have to have a readiness of mind. In other words you have to be open to what God is telling you. Then you have to do something about it

There is so much more to this so tomorrow I will go into what the Bible teaches us about how to be an overcomer. Sorry this was just a teaser but these posts are getting so long and I don't want to bore you too much.

In the meantime study the scriptures with a mind open to the things of God.

What Does the Bible Say?

Stand and be quiet

Yesterday I started sharing what God had given me about how to overcome when you're swallowed up by depression and despondency. First thing of course is to search the Scriptures daily.(Acts 17:11) Now to continue the journey God took me on.

What does the Bible teach us?

-To be an overcomer STAND and BE QUIET

Sometimes standing still is all you've got. The Israelites love to compare how wonderful they had an Egypt when they were slaves. Do we do that to God?

It might look as if the enemy will soon have you down for the count but sometimes what our enemy and we haven't counted on is the God we serve. Right before the children of Israel crossed the Red Sea they were ready to go back to the bondage God had liberated them from.

Aren't we just like that?

Exodus 14:13-14
"And Moses said unto the people, Fear ye not, stand still, and see the salvation of the Lord, which he will shew to you to day: For the Egyptians who ye have seen today, ye shall see them again no more forever. The Lord shall fight for you, and ye shall hold your peace."

Think about this? Can you imagine never seeing your enemy again?

NEVER!!!!

The other part of this, well actually both parts get me into trouble. I hate standing still but the next part is near impossible for me. Being quiet always gets me into trouble.

Why do we not want to be quiet and listen to his still small voice. When I listen to that voice I learn so much. He's always right on time. Even when I think he's late he's on time.

Today I'll leave you with this last thought from Jeremiah.

Jeremiah 29:11
"For I know the thoughts that I think toward you, saith the LORD, thoughts of peace, and not of evil, to give you an expected end."

Tomorrow and probably for the next few days I'll continue to take you on this journey with me. God really talked to me a lot about this. I hope it helps you as much as it has helped me.

When it is time to head to the house of God it is time to go. No matter what kind of aches, physical pains, spiritual pains and heart pains from family hurts the house of God is where you will find refuge and encouragement for your spiritual soul! So get up, get dressed and even if you'll be late GO!

JESUS IS WAITING!

When you make the effort when you don't feel like it is when you are surprised by what you receive. Just read what happened to me that morning when I made the effort.

Church this morning was beyond amazing. I walked into the Holy of Holies. It was just me and my God!

I'm headed back for Round Two of a Super Bowl with God! Nothing remotely touches what I feel in the presence of God.

Turn off the Super Bowl and find a Sunday Night Apostolic Church Service. Now, that is truly a SUPER BOWL!!!

Be Determined!

Determined means having made a firm decision and being resolved not to change it.

The Bible tells us to be determined. I Corinthians 9:24 *"Know ye not that they which run in a race run all, but one receive it the prize? So run, that ye may obtain."*

This passage is talking about our Christian walk. It is encouraging us to run the race so that we may obtain the prize of being with Jesus.

Take a look at a couple of Bible greats who had this kind of determination. First, let's take a look at Daniel in Daniel 1:8, *"But Daniel purposed in his heart that he would not defile himself with the portion of the Kings meat, nor with the wine which he drank:..."*

Can you imagine how hard that was? For most of us we wouldn't even try. It doesn't matter how hard it is for us to be determined it is something we must do if we truly want to know what it feels like to be an overcomer.

Now to Isaiah in Isaiah 50:7 where it says, *."For the Lord God will help me; therefore shall I not be confounded: therefore have I set my face like a flint, and I know that I shall not be ashamed."*

When we get truly determined it won't matter what trial or what valley comes our way we will not waver. The storm will buffet us but determination keeps us on course with God. That is when our minds are already made up.

That's when you simply say I know that I know that I know that my God has this. I know He's in control. It doesn't matter what it looks like. You just have to know that you know!

When you get to that point you're different, you've changed.

You've gone deeper in God than you ever dreamed. So, today, get determined that no matter what comes your way you will not change unless it's to grow deeper in God.

You must have PASSION!

Passion means intense, driving, or overmastering feeling or conviction; or strong and barely controllable emotion.

God keeps expanding my thoughts on how to be an overcomer. This journey could take days as I discover more God wants me to know.

Numbers 13:30 says, *"And Caleb stilled the people before Moses, and said, Let us go up at once, and possess it; for we are well able to overcome it."*

Caleb had a passion that we need to get ahold of in our spiritual journey. No matter what others thought, he stood against the crowd. He not only said they were able to come overcome it but he said they were well able to overcome it. Would you have that much conviction against your peers if there was no doubt God had told you to do something.

Ruth is another great example of someone with passion. Ruth 1:16 says, *"And Ruth said, Intreat me not to leave thee, or return from following after thee: for whither thou goest, I will go; and whither thou lodgest I will lodge: thy people shall be my people, and thy God my God."*

The last example I'm going to share this morning is straight from the mouth of Jesus in Luke 9:62
"And Jesus said unto him, No man having put his hand to the plough , and looking back is fit for the kingdom of God."

So, tell me again, Christians shouldn't be passionate. All things have to be done decently and in order. However, we have taken that to the extreme and lost passion somewhere along the road.

If we want our walk with God to be passionate our worship must be passionate. It will show in every facet of our lives. People will be drawn to us because of the Spirit of God they feel when near us.

You probably think I'm being a bit extreme. Why not? The world is extreme in shoving they're liberalism down our throats.

It's time we become extreme for Jesus. We have to stand for something or we will fall for anything. Rediscover your passion for Jesus. Then show others through love how to have a passion that not only changes you but changes those you come in contact with.

Let's not just be overcomers but passionate overcomers!

Trust God to be God

Trust means a firm belief in the reliability, truth, or strength of someone or something.

Before I even go into the passages God brought to my attention on trust I want us to stop and really think about the definition. When you think about your relationship with God how does trust affect it?

Ask yourself the following questions in relationship not only to your walk with God but in your effectiveness to being an overcomer.

1. Do you really believe that what happened in biblical times could happen today?

(For example: Elijah calling fire down to consume troops. The sea parting for Moses and the children of Israel to walk on dry ground. Think about it God being the fourth man in the fiery furnace and not a hair being singed. I could go on and on but you get the picture. Do you believe it could happen today?)

2. Do you really believe God = truth?

3. Do you believe God is reliable or do you question it because he didn't answer a prayer the way you thought he should?

4. Have you ever wondered how trusting God affected your ability to be an effective overcomer?

Now I'll take you on that journey God took me on this morning.

Proverbs 30:5
"Every word of God is pure: he is a shield unto them that put their trust in him."

Psalms 56:3-4
"What time I am afraid I will trust in thee. In God I will praise His Word, in God I have put my trust; I will not fear what flesh can do unto me."

In order to be able to say things like these two passages I've quoted we have to really trust God. It can't just be words we say. It's got to be so much more.

While studying on overcoming and everything I've gone through with depression and despondency since my husband passed away I am changed. My trust in God is at a new level.

Yes, we will all still have days when we wonder. That is called being human. But on those days you have to get a hold of yourself . Shake yourself. Take you to an altar and re-establish your trust in God.

All of us should strive to trust God with every part of our lives every day of our lives. It doesn't have to make sense. Gods economy will never make sense in our economy.

So why do we limit God and what he can do for us?

Please God

First, I think we need to have a clear understanding of the word please.

Pleasing means to cause to feel happy or satisfied.

Now, let's say that again.

To overcome you need to cause God to feel happy or satisfied.

Did you ever think about it that way? I hadn't.

In studying being an overcomer and the many different sides of it God is showing me where I have missed it. So when we are going through a valley or trial and we get stuck in depression and despondency we need to try to please God; to make him feel happy or satisfied.

Then the next question is how do you please God?

Hebrews 11:6
"But without faith it is impossible to please him:..."

Hebrews 13:16
"But to do good and to communicate forget not: for with such sacrifices God is well pleased."

Proverbs 10:5
"He that gathereth in summer is a wise son: but he that sleepeth in harvest is a son that causeth shame."

Mark 12:33
"And to love him with all the heart and all the understanding, and with all the soul, and with all the strength, and to love his neighbor as himself, is more than all whole burnt offerings and sacrifices."

Romans 12:1-2
"I beseech you therefore, brethren, by the mercies of God, that ye present your bodies a living sacrifice, holy, acceptable unto God which is your reasonable service. And be not conformed to this world but be ye transformed by the renewing of your mind, that ye may prove what is that good, and acceptable, and perfect, will of God."

II Corinthians 5:9
"For whether we labour, that, whether present or absent, we may be accepted of him."

Why is it so important to please God?

Galatians 1:10 answers that question clearly.

"For do I now persuade men or God? or do I seek to please men? For if I yet please men, I should not be the servant of Christ."

The highest calling is to be a servant of Christ. If we seek to please men over God we can't be the servant of Christ.

So in this journey you're going on with me about learning how to be an overcomer it digs in the corners of our hearts. For those of us who have never wanted to rock the boat it's hard to realize but sometimes pleasing God is the exact opposite of pleasing people. It's like this, either stand for something or fall for anything.

Anything valuable will cost you something. Going through the valley is one thing but learning how to sacrifice to come out of the valley is a whole new realm of closeness with God.

Think about it. Apply it to your life. Look at what the scriptures say. Then find yourself a place to pray.

Be joyful & rejoice in ALL things

Joyful means feeling, expressing, or causing great pleasure and happiness.

Rejoice means to feel or show great joy or delight

Here we go again. We're to cause God great pleasure and happiness, great joy and delight!

In the trial or valley you are going through how do you show not just joy but great joy or delight? All trials and valleys are hard. They are not measurable from person to person or circumstance to circumstance. It does not matter whether you are a teenager or nearing the end if your journey whatever trial or valley you are going through is big to you.

I Peter 4:12-13
"Beloved, think it not strange concerning the fiery trial which is to try you, as though some strange thing happened unto you. But rejoice, inasmuch as you are partakers of Christ's sufferings; that, when his glory shall be revealed you may be glad also with exceeding joy.

In other words why do we think we are the only one? Why do we think no one has ever been through this before? Friends may even tell us we must be doing something wrong. This must be the judgment of God. That's what they told Job.

What if?

What if in order to know exceeding joy in Jesus we have to go through certain trials?

Is it worth it?

You bet it is!

So, in our valley of despair what we must do is shake ourselves!

We must lift up holy hands and worship the one who gave all that we might have hope!

Tomorrow I will talk about joy with patience. To me those two words shouldn't even be in the same sentence. Today, even in your despair, find joy in Jesus!
****

Joy with Patience

I have had a love hate affair with the word patience. It keeps haunting me. I had never prayed for patience but it kept being tested so let's see what the Bible says about patience with joy.

Colossians 1:11

"Strengthened with all might, according to his glorious power, unto all patience and longsuffering with joyfulness;"

So, here, the Bible clearly tells us that we will be strengthened unto all patience and longsuffering with joyfulness. Think about those words for a moment. Really think about it.

I'm sitting here today just thinking about it. As I think about I realize true joy comes from patience and longsuffering. When and is in a sentence it's like a + sign. In other words they go together like a car needs gas to move. We need patience and longsuffering. But when going through our trial of longsuffering we've got to realize if we don't wallow in our sorrow we will know the true joy of the Lord in an even greater way then we ever dreamed.

That's hard to believe when you're sinking in depression and despondency but it is possible. Don't let depression wrap around you like a blanket that you go and seek comfort in. You have to throw that blanket off and realize your strength and your joy comes from God. Take your examples from the Bible.

Below are a few examples of those who were longsuffering:
1. Noah
2. Abraham
3. Moses
4. Job
5. Daniel
6. David

7. Mary
8. Peter
9. Paul
10. John

Are we any better than they were?

No.

We are all people striving to be saved just like they were. The examples they set before us teach us how to walk this way. That is why we must know our Bible and know how to go to our knees when we are going through those valley's that just keep on going for years and years.

Even in those valleys we can know joy if we get the right attitude about patience. Everything in this book boils down to us, our attitude. We have to get it and understand it for us. We have to know that God loves us. We have to be able to worship him no matter what.

I think it's time to pray.

Never ever give up!

Luke 18:1
"And he spake a parable unto them to this end, that men ought always to pray, and not faint."

Galatians 6:9
"And let us not be weary in well doing: for in due season we shall reap, if we faint not."
****

You will learn how to stand and be a true overcomer when you understand that on your knees in prayer is when you truly stand. We want things to come the easy way. As I've set in the hospital this night and dealt with many situations and memories I know God is cleaning another corner of my heart out.

It is in those times we not only need to pray but to take ourselves to the Word of God for the answers we seek about our situation(s). Then seek the Godly counsel of your pastor.

Most of the time well-meaning friends look at the situation from the outside not understanding or knowing all that is going on. What is normal in one situation may not be normal for another family.

We should not insert ourselves into situations we personally have no knowledge of unless it is to pray. If you feel you must ask others to pray it is not your right to share details of the situation when you don't have permission to do so. When asking people to pray for a specific person or family just say it is an unspoken request and leave it. Do not utter another word.

In order to understand not being weary in well doing is to first understand Jesus never got weary with us. So, no matter what the situation, no matter how unfair it may be, no matter, just no matter, remember, Jesus is still Lord of all!

Lastly, let's take an example from the apostles in the book of Acts chapter 16 verse 25. They should have given up. If it had been us, we probably would have. This verse teaches us a big lesson about what to do in the midnight hour.

"And at midnight Paul and Silas prayed, and sang praises unto God: and the prisoners heard them."

Your prayers in your midnight hour will not only affect your situation but will affect others that watch how you handle yourself as a Christian during your time of crisis. The greatest soul winning tool we have is how we live and overcome in the name of Jesus.

So, **NEVER GIVE UP!**

Tomorrow I will share the journey God has taken me on to learn how to encourage myself in the Lord.

You must learn how to
encourage yourself in the
Lord.

Encourage means to give support, confidence or hope.

In the journey God is taking me on He first took me to Job. If any book in the Bible can show us how someone who loses everything and by example shows us how to pick ourselves up with the help of God it is the book of Job. Even with his friends attack him verbally when he would respond you would find a nugget hidden here and there where he encourages himself.

\------------------------------

Job 17:9
"The righteous also shall hold on his way, and he that hath clean hands shall be stronger and stronger."

Job 19:25-27, 25
"For I know that my redeemer liveth, and that he shall stand at the latter day upon the earth." 26. "And though after skin worms destroy this body, yet in my flesh I shall see God." 27. "Whom I shall see for myself , and mine eyes shall behold, and not another, though my reins be consumed within me."

Job 42:2
"I know that thou canst do every thing, and that no thought can be withholden from thee."

\----------------------------

The way to encourage yourself in the Lord is to quote scriptures to yourself, read the Word of God and apply it to your situation along with prayer. Then remember every time God supplied your needs and rescued you.

Yes it may be a different situation but the God we serve is the same God that rescued us before and that will be there again and again.

You see, the difference between an overcomer and one who can't overcome is the fact they haven't learned how to stand on

the Word of God and its promises. We must hide the Word in our hearts so we can remember His promises to us and encourage ourselves like the greats of the Bible have done.

Let's encourage ourselves no matter our situation!

Learn how to speak
positively

A few points I will hit today and tomorrow, the most important being that it is definitely Biblical.

First, I will go to some passages that God took me to to remind me about positive thinking and speaking.

Jeremiah 29:12
"Then shall ye call upon me, and ye shall go and pray unto me, and I will hearken unto you."

Phillippians 4:13
"I can do all things through Christ which strengtheneth me."

Isaiah 55:12
"For ye shall go out with joy, and be led forth with peace: the mountains and the hills shall break forth before you into singing, and all the trees shall clap their hands."

Luke 11:9
"And I say unto you, Ask, and it will be given to you; seek, and ye shall find; knock, and it shall be opened to you."

Romans 8:28
"And we know that all things work together for good to them that love God, to them who are the called according to His purpose."

Galatians 3:9
"And if ye be Christ's, then are ye Abraham's seed and heirs according to the promise."

Secondly, today, God wants to remind me and you that we are His!

Because we are His we need to understand that our thoughts need to change. Yes, bad things happen to us but it's what we allow those things to do to us that are the real problem.

When we learn how to stand on the promises of God in our mind and to speak to our situations that's when we will see real change within ourselves.

It is important that you understand this is not a get out of jail free card for those situations we put ourselves into. God will rescue us even out of those situations. It is, however, important to realize how changing our way of thinking will realign us to being so much closer to our God.

You and I need to learn to speak to our situation! We need to remind the devil who our God is!

Most of the time it's not the devil who is the problem but us. That is when we simply need to remind ourselves who our God is!

Today speak and think positively to yourself. Then if you are like me you might need to repent for your thoughts about what God could or could not do in your situation.

****

Think and Speak Positively

Why is it so important to think and speak positively?

The Bible tells us why.

Proverbs 18:21
"Death and life are in the power of the tongue: and they that love it shall eat the fruit thereof."

Ps. 27:13
"I had fainted, unless I had believed to see the goodness of the Lord in the land of the living."

Philippians 2:5
"Let this mind be in you, which was also in Christ Jesus."

Psalms 50:15
"And call upon me in the day of trouble: I will deliver thee, and thou shalt glorify me."

The Bible is so rich and full on this subject. We tend to shy away from those who speak about positive thinking because so many have taken it to an extreme to justify a rich lifestyle that may or may not have anything to do with Jesus. In reality positive thinking on a spiritual side has so many benefits.

----

1. Positive thinkers don't see problems as problems but as a way to build faith. They see things as they should be not as they are.

Heb. 11:1
"Now faith is the substance of things hoped for, the evidence of things not seen. "

2. Positive thinkers because of a change of thinking from negative to positive do just as Jesus taught. Then doubt leaves.

Matthew 21:21
"Jesus answered and said unto them, verily I say unto you, if ye have faith and doubt not, ye shall not only do this which is done to the fig tree, but also if ye shall say to this mountain, Be thou removed and be thou cast into the sea; it shall be done."

3. Positive thinkers speak positively thereby receiving positive results.

Proverbs 18:21 (partial quote)
"Death and life are in the power of the tongue:"

I'm only going into three bullet points here but there are so many more. You really should study this on your own and let God speak to you about your situation.

I really believe that positive thinking and positive speaking are so important in our walk with God. So when those times come when things seemingly aren't going our way remember to find the silver lining in the cloudy days.

Yes, we will have trials, valleys, and challenges but if we learn how to look up and say, God I know beyond a shadow of a doubt that you got this it will change your outlook on the problem. Once our outlook is changed we are ripe for a miracle.

Whatever we need, no matter how big or small God will provide. So when you go to pray remember the scriptures above. Sometimes when it is hard for me to be positive I pray the quoted scripture. That will build your faith.

More of Jesus, less of me
until it is all about Jesus!

This was written on Valentine's Day. It is a day we give gifts to those that we love. What greater gift could we give Jesus then to give Him us?

What I mean is by doing what we sing about all the time. Remember, "I will give you all, I will not withhold." By giving Him all so that our lives truly become all about Him so that we are no longer holding anything back.

Let's see what the Bible says:

Galatians 2:20
"I am crucified with Christ: nevertheless I live; yet not I, but Christ liveth in me: and the life which I now live in the flesh I live by the faith of the Son of God, who loved me, and gave himself for me."

Galatians 5:24-25
"And they that are Christ's have crucified the flesh with the affections and lusts. If we live in the Spirit, let us also walk in the Spirit."

II Corinthians 5:15
"And that He died for all, that they which live should not henceforth live unto themselves, but unto Him which died for them and rose again."

Romans 14:7-9
"For none of us liveth to himself, and no man dieth to himself. For whether we live, we live unto the Lord; and whether we die, we die unto the Lord: whether we live therefore, or die, we are the Lord's. For to this end Christ both died, and rose, and revived, that He might be Lord both of the dead and living."

There is so much more in the Bible about this. When we really get it our lives will be revolutionized for Jesus. That is when it will be all about Him.

This is not an easy process. This is not for the faint of heart. . This process requires sacrifice. The most important sacrifice we will ever give is in giving of ourselves to Jesus, complete and whole, holding back nothing.

As a very wise person once told me you think you have sacrificed everything and you haven't yet scratched the surface. Look at what you sacrificed. Now, look at what Jesus and the apostles sacrificed.

I think it's time we pray, really pray. And this time we need to really mean the words to that song, "I will give you all, I will not withhold."

Tomorrow I will share part of the journey God has taken me on about Him truly being first in my life.

God must be first!

First means coming before ALL others in time or order.

I could not begin to tell you how many messages I have heard preached on this specific subject. The Bible is very clear on this. We can rationalize our priorities anyway we wish. However, if we truly want to have the overcoming spirit that we should God will be first in our lives.

Let's see what the Bible has to say about this.

Exodus 20:3
"Thou shalt have no other gods before me."

Matthew 6:33
"But seek ye first the kingdom of God, and His righteousness; and all these things shall be added unto you.

I believe these two verses make it crystal clear that God must be first. If God is not first we could have made some of those things God blessed us with gods in our life. When we put God first we will have a different mindset about the things of God and the work of God.

Below are a couple of more passages that will give you the idea of what Jesus meant when he spoke and of how the apostles interpreted it.

Matthew 8:21-22
"And another of his disciples said unto him, Lord, suffer me first to go and bury my father. But Jesus said unto him, follow me and let the dead bury their dead."

Romans 8:5

"For they that are after the flesh do mind the things of the flesh but they that are after the Spirit the things of the Spirit."

What do these passages mean?

I am a very simplistic person when it comes to the Scriptures. I believe it means what it says it means. Sometimes the Bible in the words of Jesus are very strong and hard to understand because of the emphasis we put on things today that are not of the Spirit.

We have to get it!

We really have to get it! We don't have time to play! People are dying and going to hell because we, as Christians, refuse to put God first. We have every excuse in the book.

We can't help out because the house needs cleaned; the kids have activities (not church or God related); we say we cannot spend time in the prayer room before church because the kids will act up; and our excuses go on and on. Well, those kids God blessed you with will never learn how important prayer and a close relationship with God is unless you teach them by example.

Yes, they will act up. However, what you are teaching them every time you take them to a prayer room or a place of prayer is how to enter into the presence of God. After a while they will learn and start having their own conversations with God because they watched you put Him first in all things and not just on Sunday.

When you put God first everything else will just automatically fall into place as long as you do it with the right attitude. Don't put your family last. They come next after God. You love them as Christ loved the church.

So, today, let's examine our priorities and see where God is in that list. If He is not first in your life your priorities need realigned to the Word of God.

Is He Lord of all or not Lord at all?

Cast your cares upon him

DO NOT WORRY!

I can already hear you. What do you know about my problems? You don't have a clue what I'm going through. I have uttered those same words.

Yes, unfortunately, I do have a clue what you're going through and so do many others because we've all had to go through things we never dreamed in our wildest nightmares.

Here's a partial list of some of those things I have dealt with
1) Cancer
2) Financial crisis
3) Lost love
4) Drugs
5) Backslidden family

And many other problems have visited our families.

Do not think that just because we are Christians we have a get out of jail free card. The difference between someone who understands overcoming and someone who doesn't is how we allow these problems to affect our futures.

First, let's define a couple of words. These two words are very important to people who want to be an overcomer. I believe we must understand exactly what the Bible tells us to do. All the definitions I have looked up online.

Worry is to give way to anxiety or unease; allow one's mind to dwell on difficulty or troubles.

Cast is to throw forcefully in a specified direction.

What does the Bible tell us to do about our problems, our worries?

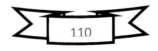

I Peter 5:7
"Casting all your care upon Him, for He careth for you."

Phillippians 4:6
"Be careful for nothing; but in every thing by prayer and supplication with thanksgiving let your requests be made known unto God."

Psalms 55:22
"Cast thy burden upon the Lord,.."

None of this is easy to do. That's why some get stuck in depression and despondency while others learn how to overcome in the same situations. We all learn at different speeds. Some of us have to revisit the same lesson again and again. I, for one, am ready to move on and get this.

When we get this then we will understand no matter how big our problems are, our God is bigger! When we worry we are taking God's responsibility away from him.

He wants to take care of our problems and our needs for us but we have to learn how to give those problems and needs to him. We have to cast those problems in the opposite direction from us towards our God and let Him handle them.

Yes, we have to live through it. However, when we know he's taking care of it for us it relieves us as much as we will allow it to.

When we cast our cares on Him Matthew 7:11 makes sense to us.

"If ye then, being evil, I know how to give good gifts until your children, how much more shall your father which is in heaven give good things to them that ask him?"

It is so important that we get it. In our walk with God we have to realize that he is our Father. He only wants to help us. Sometimes we have to go through valleys to grow. While in the valley we have to listen to his still small voice.

While in that valley sometimes there is so much noise from others who think they know what God is doing. Sometimes the voices get too much. That's when you go off alone, like Jesus, and pray. Plead the blood over your mind so that you will know the voice of God and not the voices of people. Remember God will never tell you to go against His Word.

Tomorrow, I will share the journey God is taking me on about how we discourage others without realizing it. True overcomers don't discourage others, they encourage them.

Do not discourage others

Discourage is to make (someone) less determined, hopeful, confident; or to deprive of confidence, hope or spirit

----

Have you done this?

Have I done this?

Let's see what the Bible has to say about this?

Numbers 32:6-7
"And Moses said unto the children of Gad and to the children of Reuben, Shall your brethren go to war, and shall ye sit here? And wherefore discourage ye the heart of the children of Israel from going over into the land which the Lord hath given them?"

Job 16:1-7
"Then Job answered and said, I have heard many such things: miserable conforters are ye all. Shall vain words have an end? Or what emboldenest thee that thou answerest. I also could speak as ye do if your soul were in my souls stead, I could heap up words against you, and shake mine head at you. But I would strengthen you with my mouth, and the moving of my lips should asswage your grief. Though I speak, my grief is not asswaged: and though I forbear, what am I eased. But now he hath made me weary: thou hast made desolate all my company."

Have you or I discouraged someone from following the will of God for their life?

Can you imagine with me, yourself or members of your family, being mentioned in the Bible as miserable comforters. In other

words they were discouragers. How many messages have we heard preached on being like Bildad, Eliphaz, Zophar or Job's wife?

Precisely my point! That is why we do not know who they were because they were miserable comforters. They had no clue what the word encourage meant but they had an extremely close relationship with the word discourage.

This is why it is so important to think before we speak. Have you or I been a miserable comforter to someone?

Now, let's see what the Bible tells us we should do.

Ephesians 4:29
"Let no corrupt communication proceed out of your mouth, but that which is good to the use of edifying, that it may minister grace unto the hearers."

Think about this for a minute. If you are a discourager is your communication corrupt?

Tomorrow I will take you on the journey God took me on about the importance of being an encourager.

Be an encourager

Encourage is to give support, confidence or hope

Edify is to instruct or improve (someone) morally or intellectually

----

It is not just good enough to be able to encourage yourself in the Lord when you're depressed or despondent. A true overcomer can encourage others when their own world is falling apart before their eyes. You think that is impossible. I did too until I learned how to let God have complete control (most of the time, however, I am still very human).

During the past almost 6 months and today God has sent people into my path from the American Cancer Society, the Pancreatic Cancer Action Network, to just mention a few of the professional organizations I work with to encourage people who are fighting for their lives. Barring a miracle these people are battling illnesses that typically will take their lives.

Today, when I make the call to encourage that person I received a phone call about yesterday I have to be able to step out of my situation and into theirs. I can't let my problems bleed into what I tell them.

True overcomers can put their problems to the side and focus on the person they have to encourage. They need help. No matter who comes to you needing hope you have to forget your problems for a little while to give them hope.

You'll find when you do this you give yourself hope. You think it's a play on words. It is not. That is just how it works. The Bible teaches us that but that's not why. I do it. I simply do it because I love to help people. We should all love to help others and love like Jesus.

Joshua 1:9
"Have not I commanded thee? Be strong and of a good courage; be not afraid, neither be thou dismayed: for the LORD thy God is with thee whithersoever thou goest."

I Thessalonians 5:11
"Wherefore comfort yourselves together, and edify one another, even as also ye do."

Romans 15:4
"For whatsoever things were written aforetime were written for our learning, that we through patience and comfort of the Scriptures might have hope."

Knowing the Word of God is a big key to being able to encourage others when our world continues to fall apart. Remember Philippians 4:8 when you start to focus on your problems. You'll find within those words encouragement and blessing.

"Finally, brethren, whatsoever things are true, whatsoever things are honest, whatsoever things are just, whatsoever things are pure, whatsoever things are lovely, whatsoever things are of good report; of there be any virtue, and if there be any praise, think on these things."
******

comfort others

Why should we comfort others?

That's a simple answer. It's because the Bible instructs us to do this.

Isaiah 40:1
"Comfort ye, comfort ye my people."

Romans 1:12
"That is, that I may be comforted together with you by the mutual faith both of you and me."

II Corinthians 1:3-4
"Blessed be God, even the Father of our Lord Jesus Christ, the Father of mercies, and the God of all comfort; who comforteth us in all our tribulation, that we may be able to comfort them which are in any trouble, by the comfort wherewith we ourselves are comforted of God."

I think that's pretty plain. In Romans God lets us know by comforting others we are comforted with mutual faith.

Lastly, we find that God is the God of all comfort. He comforts us so we can then comfort others as He has comforted us.

So, today, when you see someone who needs comfort, comfort them. Let them see Jesus in you through everything you do. Make time in your busy schedule to comfort someone.

Let God comfort you when
you can't comfort yourself

Have you ever felt like there was no hope? I know I have. Let's check out Jeremiah.

Jeremiah 1:8
"When I would comfort myself against sorrow, my heart is faint in me."

This is a normal human feeling. It's not in feeling of losing hope that is the problem. It's in what we allow this to do to us.

I know, you want me to explain myself. Okay, I will. What God talked to me about through this with my own grief and lost hope went like this.

So, I've given you great blessings, miracles, and so much more that you can't even count in your little mind. Yet you sit there wallowing in self-pity. It's time to get up off your butt and do something for me!

In the beginning of my grief process God's comfort was gentle arms wrapped around me. Because this continued for several months that's when God's comfort changed. Sometimes we need a wake-up call to get us up. A jolt of reality from God talking to us is what we need to get us going.

Let's see what the Bible tells us about God comforting us.

II Thessalonians 2:16-17
"Now our Lord Jesus Christ himself, and God, even our father, which hath loved us, and hath given us everlasting consolation and good hope through grace, Comfort your hearts, and stablish you in every good word and work."

Psalms 147:3
"He healeth the broken in heart, and bindeth up their wounds."

John 14:18
"I will not leave you comfortless: I will come to you."

Remember, today, God's comfort is there but after a while we have to learn how to comfort ourselves in the Word of God.

So, today, get up, brush yourself off, memorize some encouraging scriptures to quote to yourself when depression and despondency come knocking. Then you, with the help of God, can send depression and despondency packing!

Tomorrow I will take you on the journey God took me on about starting to move for Him.

****

Move!

Did you ever stop to think that what you perceive to be your biggest obstacle could in fact become your way to overcome? Last night as I was lying in the hospital and they were running tests and I felt God talk to me more about this spiritually. So let me take you on the highlights of the journey God took me on.

Define move
Go in a specified direction or manner; change position.

Define walk
Move at a regular and fairly slow pace, by lifting and setting down each foot in turn, never having both feet off the ground at once.

Genesis 13:17
"Arise, walk through the land in the length of it and in the breadth of it; for I will give it unto thee."

Exodus 13:15
"And the LORD said unto Moses, wherefore criest thou unto me? Speak unto the children of Israel, that they go forward."

Daniel 3:25
"He answered and said. Lo, I see four men loose, walking in the midst of the fire, and they have no hurt; and the form of the fourth is like the Son of God."

Matthew 14:29
"And He said, Come. And when Peter was come down out of the ship, he walked on the water, to go to Jesus."

John 5:8
"Jesus saith unto him, Rise, take up thy bed, and walk."

Acts 17:28
"For in Him we live, and move, and have our being; as certain also of your own poets have said, For we are also His offspring."

The same type of crisis can happen to two different people with two very different outcomes. The outcome is based on the response of a person to the crisis.

Overcomers don't see a crisis as a crisis but they see it as a bump in the road. They feel that this bump in the road that God is with them. That's why when you look at the passages of Scripture God led me to above you see people's responses and then you see God's response.

When God told Peter to come and walk on the water he could have refused. If he had refused he would have missed one of the greatest miracles of his life. Because he obeyed he literally walked on water.

It's the same with us. I could go on and on there are so many examples but think about the ones I have above. Sometimes it is hard when you're the one laying in a hospital bed. An overcomer is one whose trust is in God and knows that their trust is just simply in God no matter what.

I want to define one more word.

Stagnant is having no current or flow and often having an unpleasant smell as a consequence.

What you need to do today is look at yourself and the problems you've had. How have you dealt with them? Have you included God in every aspect of your life? Do you overcome your problems or do you allow your problems to overcome you? Do problems and crisis stop you?

When you do look at the definition above of stagnant and apply it to yourself you will have to change. As Christians we should not be stagnant. We should move and flow in the presence of God. We should not stink in the presence of God or be unmoved.

Lastly let's go to one more scripture.

II CORINTHIANS 5:7, "(For we walk by faith, not by sight:)"

Think about it. Examine your own life. Let the Bible talk to you. Let it change you. No matter what situation we have in our lives we simply walk by faith.

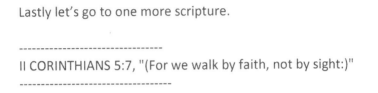

Have a Testimony

How do you get a testimony?

Well, you have to have a test.

First, let's look at the definition of testimony as found on dictionary.com.

Testimony
1. the statement or declaration of a witness under oath or affirmation, usually in court.
2. evidence in support of a fact or statement; proof.
3. open declaration or profession, as of faith.

Looking at this definition God is showing me that I can't produce evidence if I have never been through anything. In order to share what God can do we have to go through some things.

Let's look at what the Bible has to say about a testimony. The Bible tells us what we're supposed to do with ours.

Psalms 81:5
"This he ordained in Joseph for a testimony, when he went out through the land of Egypt: where I heard a language that I understood not."

Mark 5:19
"Howbeit, Jesus suffered him not, but saith unto him, go home to thy friends, and tell them how great things the Lord has done for thee and have had compassion on thee."

Luke 21:12-14
"But before all these, they shall lay their hands on you, and persecute you, delivering you up to the synagogue, and into prisons being brought before kings and rulers for my name's sake. And it shall turn to you for a testimony. Settle it therefore in your hearts, not to meditate before what ye shall answer."

So, think about the tribulations of Joseph as below:
1) Went from being the favored son to thrown into a pit
2) Sold into slavery
3) Became a servant
4) Falsely accused
5) Thrown into prison

After the tests he was recognized. This was always a part of God's plan for his life. Let's calmly take a look at our own life.

Could it all be part of a bigger purpose?

If you have a testimony of God doing great things in your life and you never share it are you disobeying God?

There are so many people that need encouraged. Have you ever thought that your testimony could be life changing for someone else? Perhaps bring them to God.

It is time we quit hiding our light under a bushel and share it with others! So no matter what situation you may find yourself in look for an opportunity to share the greatness of our God.

Tomorrow, I will take you on the journey God took me on about the value of our individual testimonies to God.

What is the value of your
testimony to God?

Define Value:
1. the regard that something is held to deserve; the importance, worth, or usefulness of something
2. a person's principles or standards of behavior; one's judgment of what is important in life.

In the journey God took me on about the value of our individual testimonies I have been overwhelmed at the value God places on them. In Exodus we see it where it is referring to the tablets of the covenant. However, those tablets were a testimony given to Moses from God. Think about that. God was teaching us by example.

Exodus 25:16
"And thou shalt put into the ark the testimony which I shall give thee."

Exodus 30:6
"And thou shalt put it before the vail that is by the ark of the testimony, before the mercy seat that is over the testimony, where I will meet with thee."

Look where it is placed. It is placed before the veil that is by the ark of the testimony but before the mercy seat that is over the testimony. Then God says I will meet you there. I am still trembling when I think of this. So if you don't think your testimony is valuable think about the example God Himself gave us by what He did so that we would know.

I am not a great Bible Scholar. I am a very simple person when it comes to this. However, it awes me to know how much God values our testimonies. Another example is Job 1:8. You see God knew Job's testimony.

I wonder does He know your testimony?

Does Jesus know my testimony?

Job 1:8,
"And the Lord said unto Satan, Hast thou considered my servant Job, that there is none like him in the earth, a perfect and an upright man, one that feareth God and escheweth evil?"

Do we have this testimony before God?

I think it's time to examine some more of those dark corners in our heart we hold in reserve just for us. All of our hearts have to be given to Him. No Holding Back if we truly want to have a testimony like Job that God would use him as an example to the devil.

Tomorrow I will continue to take you on the journey God has taken me on about our testimonies by sharing with you the benefits a testimony gives us when we share it

Benefits of Having a Testimony

A benefit is an advantage or profit gained from something

Think about that definition in relationship to your walk with God. To have a testimony you have benefits. I know it doesn't seem that way when you're being tested but oh, the relationship when you learn how to depend on God for everything.

Did you ever think that having a test has a great benefit to you as a Christian?

Let's see what the Bible has to say about it.

\---

Job 2:3
"And the Lord said unto Satan, Hast thou considered my servant Job, that there is none like him in the earth, a perfect and an upright man, one that feareth God and escheweth evil? And still he holdeth fast his integrity, although thou movedst against him to destroy him without cause."

Psalms 19:7
"The law of the Lord is perfect, converting the soul: the testimony of the Lord is sure making wise the simple."

Hebrews 11:5
"By faith Enoch was translated that he should not see death; and was not found because God had translated him: for before his translation he had this testimony, that he pleased God."

Revelation 12:11
"And they overcame him by the blood of the Lamb, and by the word of their testimony; and they loved not their lives unto the death."

\---

Five things I see in these four passages as benefits of your test and testimony:

1) You keep your integrity before God.
2) You have a testimony before God.
3) Testimony of the Lord makes wise the simple.
4) You please God.
5) You overcome by the word of your testimony.

Just think about these benefits!

WOW!

As I am reading these passages I kept getting more and more excited about my relationship with God and my testimony. I'm nothing great just a normal everyday person. Most of the people in the Bible didn't think of themselves as anything extraordinary. It's not in being extraordinary it's in not letting situations or circumstances define your outcome but letting your walk with God define the outcome.

I want to be the one like Enoch that had the testimony that he pleased God. I don't care about pleasing men. I just want to please God.

So today, if you're being tested, count yourself blessed and highly favored of God. Then look at what you can accomplish with your testimony. You never know how many lives your test will ultimately help and touch if you learn how to be a victor instead of always a victim.

Praise God in your valley!

Watch Him do miraculous things in your life. Sometimes the process is slow and sometimes it is fast but however long your valley is to know that Jesus is with you and on Him you can depend. **Let's be Victors not Victims!**

You must be a giver

I can hear you already thinking she's going to talk about offering and tithes. That is required Biblically and useful but not where I'm going this morning. God talked to me about being a giver to others to truly overcome in my own life.

Let's see where God took me on this journey through the Bible on giving.

Acts 20:35
"I have shewed you all things, how that so laboring ye ought to support the weak, and to remember the words of the Lord Jesus, how he said it is more blessed to give than to receive."

II Cor 9:6
"But this (I say), He which soweth sparingly shall reap also sparingly; and he which soweth bountifully shall reap also bountifully."

We have all heard it seemingly a million times, *"it is more blessed to give than to receive"*. It is so important to understand the concept of giving no matter our situation or circumstances.

We have to quit focusing on our problems and learn how to focus on others. Not only will this help others but it will ultimately help us more. I've found when I reach out to help someone whether it's to bless them with something or my time to encourage them I usually walk away having received more than I gave.

To receive is not the reason to give. We should give simply because that's what we should do.

No matter what your situation today find someone you can give to. Everyone has something to give.

Watch and see how it will change your life!

Tomorrow I will talk about the journey God has taken me on about how to give Biblically to be an overcomer.

Give according to the Bible.

Giving according to the Bible is very important.

Below are the Biblical requirements for how to give:
1) Give in secret.
2) Give as God has purposed in your heart.
3) Give abundantly.
4) Give cheerfully.

God brought these three points to my mind this morning from the following three scriptures. Come on this journey with me that God is taking me on.

Matthew 6:1-4
"Take heed that ye do not your alms before men, to be seen of them: otherwise you have no reward of your father which is in heaven. Therefore when thou doest thine alms, do not sound a trumpet before thee, as the hypocrites do in the synagogues and the streets, that they may have glory of men. Verily I say unto you, They have their reward. That thine alms may be in secret: and thy Father which seeth in secret himself shall reward thee openly. "

Luke 6:38
"Give and it shall be given unto you: good measure pressed down, and shaken together, and running over, shall men give unto your bosom. For with the same measure that ye mete withal that shall be measured to you again."

II Corinthians 9:7
"Every man according as he purposeth in his heart, (so let him give); not grudgingly, or of necessity: for God loveth a cheerful giver."

True overcomers learn how. They apply themselves to wanting to have the mind of Christ. This is usually unpopular especially among Americans. We want the easy way out. The easy way out is not how you get close to God.

As we have heard said many times if you don't stand for something you will fall for anything. So, when you sing, "I will give you all, I will not withhold," think about those words and what they really mean.

If God should ask of you all will you do it? Not only that but will you do it with a smile?

Don't be upset. God will bless you. God will take care of you. Think about your giving and what God has asked of you. Have you done what He asked?

FORGIVE

We like to say we know how to forgive. I tend to think we don't have a clue. We say we forgive people for things they've done to us. However, in a moment of anger we bring it all back up. God has talked to me this morning about my journey on being an overcomer and about true forgiveness.

(1) define the word forgive.
----

    a) To give up resentment of or claim requital for (forgive an insult).

    b) To cease to feel resentment against(an offender).

I want you to really think about your relationships and the people who have hurt you right now. No matter what happens in life usually a person is behind the problems that we have. It's not in the problem it's in how we deal with the problems.

Now, I need you to think about definitions in relationship to that. Now we're going to go on the journey God took me on through the Bible. At least a small look at what God is showing me.

2. Reading God's mind on forgiveness.

Matthew 6:14-15
"For if ye forgive men their trespasses, your heavenly Father will also forgive you: But if you forgive not men their trespasses, neither will your Father forgive your trespasses."

Ephesians 4:32
"And be ye kind one to another, tenderhearted, forgiving one another, even as God for Christ's sake hath forgiven you."

Mark 11:25-26
"And when you stand praying, forgive, if ye have a ought against any: that your father which is in heaven may forgive you your trespasses. But if ye do not forgive, neither will your Father which is in heaven forgive your trespasses."

----

3. Summation of the passages from my viewpoint:
These passages of Scripture are pretty clear about forgiveness. We have to forgive, really forgive. When you really forgive you don't continue to bring it back up.

Yes, it may affect your future relationship with that person because of past situations. But we have to get where we truly have forgiven. That means you don't hold it against them. If God held everything against us that we had done we wouldn't be allowed in the church.

4. Let's look at how many times God expects us to forgive.

Matthew 18:21-22
"Then came Peter to him, and said, Lord, how oft shall my brother sin against me, and I forgive him? til seven times? Jesus saith unto him, I say not until thee, until seven times but until seventy times seven."

----

5. Our need to forgive and the need to be forgiven.

It is a given people will hurt us. What we don't know is how we will deal with it. Overcomers understand the principles of forgiveness because they've been forgiven as much as all have.

I know I need to forgive. Over the past years I have suffered hurts I could have never imagined before from people who are very dear to my heart. I still love them but some days I have to work at forgiving them.

Forgiveness is essential to living for God. We need it and we need to get it. Prayer and knowing the mind of God is the key that unlocks the door to forgiveness.

In this section of forgiveness as I was working on the proof this morning God impressed me to open up a little more about how I am dealing with forgiveness in my own life.

My loving husband who encouraged me to follow the call of God took his own life and robbed myself and my children of a future with him by our sides. I have to forgive him. Many of us have to forgive people who have wronged us that are no longer with us.

How do we do this?

Well, we have to go and talk to them. For me that has been two visits to his grave questioning him as to why. Yes, I know he cannot answer me. It's not answers from him I will ever get but I have to get the anger out and then work on me to get to the root of bitterness that tries to rear its ugly head every so often.

In order to be forgiven my Bible teaches me I must first forgive. Has my life been perfect? No. Will anyone's life ever be perfect? No. Are people reading this book who have been physically and sexually molested. Yes.

Do you have to forgive those who have harmed you?

My Bible teaches me that you do.

Will this be easy?

No. Will you hate me for telling you that you have to forgive them. Yes.

Below are some text messages that were sent late at night to someone extremely dear to me who had unthinkable things required of her as a child that make us cringe. We think we have it hard but we have no idea how hard some have it.

When you see people try to look beyond the way they are dressed or the way they speak. Bitterness and hatred come from much hurt. We have to take care that we don't become like that when things happen to us we could not have dreamed in our worst nightmares.

> *"How do you feel about your mom helping a teenage girl out of her situation?"*

> *"Wow, no one has asked me that."*

> *"Knowing what I know, loving you, of course, I had to ask how you feel."*

> *"I don't know there's so much she could have done for me and she didn't I don't know how much you know about my life but my dad put me on the street with my mom to turn tricks. She could have stopped that."*

> *"Why didn't she?"*

> *"Why didn't she?"*

> *"I don't know it's weird all of it."*

> *"Yes, I knew. I don't have an answer for you. I wish I did."*

> *"I do agree it's strange."*

"I will be praying for you. I love you. I so wish there was something I could have done back then to have stopped your nightmare from coming to life."

"Thanks."

"How do I forgive them?"

"Do I?"

"Do I have to?"

"It will not be easy but you have to forgive them. Otherwise it will stand between you and God. Why, you wonder, do you have to forgive something so terrible, so horribly unexplainable?"

"Well, first, because the Bible tells us in Matthew 6:15:
> *'But if ye forgive not men their trespasses, neither will your father forgive your trespasses.'"*

"This is Jesus talking in the Bible. What you have to remember is that you aren't forgiving them for them. You have to forgive them so that you can be forgiven."

"Also by holding onto all that anger, hurt, and hate (I'm sure there is hate involved because I would hate them). It causes bitterness and anger."

"Thanks, no one has ever put it like that..."

"I so wish I could see you more to help me get closer to God... I don't know how."

"I wish I could see you more also. I want to help you. I want to be there. I need to clone me... Now there's a scary thought for you."

"To be closer to God you really have to work on forgiving both of them."

"Let me tell you how I start my day. Every morning I get up and read my Bible. If you really want to know God, who He is, and how He operates you will get into the Bible. One minister told me the Bible is the mind of God."

"I started by reading four pages a day and if I was really interested in what I was reading I would continue until I was tired but no less than four pages a day. That was doable."

"Then I take me (a lot of days I physically have to take me) to my knees and pray. It's not easy but it is so worth it."

"And then there's that, Lord, I don't know what to say when I pray."

"Let me share with you how I pray. First I thank God for all His blessings on me. For example: my ministry (job), health, family, home, automobiles, safety, beautiful day,

food to eat, and so forth. No matter the situation there is plenty to be thankful for."

"I do that, though, my mind usually wonders A LOT!"

"Everyone's mind wanders, that's normal."

"Next, after I worship Him, I repent. I sin a lot. I am so human, LOL."

"I ask for forgiveness for me. I want to be as clean as I can be before Him. There are so many things I have to repent for every day."

"Well, you don't drink, smoke or cuss so what do you have to repent?"

"Sin is sin whether it is smoking, cussing, gossiping, murder, speeding, and so on. All have to be repented of. When it comes to asking for forgiveness.... Well the devil makes sure I know what mistakes I have made... LOL."

"After I repent, it is then I bring my needs to God. I also bring my family's needs, my friend's needs and so on. I lay those needs at His feet letting Him know that I know that He can take care of anything and everything I have need of."

"A lady at my church told me she has a list she reads through every night of her prayers."

"A list would be helpful but once you do it several times it will become second nature to you. That's when you will find yourself just doing it."

"Lastly in prayer before I finish I always worship God again for all He has done. When you see me posting songs on facebook it's songs I have listened to while I was praying. By the way in getting closer to God Acts 2:38 can be very helpful. I firmly believe this verse is for us today.

> *'Then Peter said unto them, Repent, and be baptized every one of you in the name of Jesus Christ for the remission of your sins, and ye shall receive the gift of the Holy Ghost.'"*

So, today, you're depressed and have many situations in your life. Who do you need to forgive? When we forgive we must forget. We have to quit bringing it up. This could take many trips to our knees and our Bibles to get there.

I have seen many people struggle with true forgiveness. True forgiveness goes hand in hand with putting the wrong under the blood and walking away from it. Some people will never ask you for forgiveness. You are not forgiving them because they ask. You are forgiving them because it stands between you and God.

I want you to realize this does not mean you have to go back and let that person verbally, physically or sexually assault you again. Boundaries have to be set to protect you. With prayer and getting into your Bible you will find wisdom to help you in your situation.

I am a firm believer in going to your pastor for counsel and in seeking professional Christian counseling. I have gone to counseling and in the future should I need it I would not hesitate to seek it.

Someday I may write a book on forgiveness but for now realize it's so important you get everything out of the way so that you establish a clear communication line between you and God. I know I'm repeating a few things in this again and again but it is so important that we get this.

I don't want bitterness from a past wrong to stand as a roadblock between God and I. Those roots of hurt, bitterness, anger, disgust and dismay have to be rooted up. This will not be easy but you and I can do it. Will I have more trips to my husband's grave? I hope not but if I need to physically go there to talk to him to root out the anger and bitterness I will.

I never want anything to come between me and my relationship with God. You have to get to that point. When you do your relationship with God will change. You will find such peace and joy. One day you will wake up and the depression will be lifted.

There is so much more about overcomers but this book is a start. Another book will be coming soon focused on the promises to overcomers.

A closing note from the Author

The things that have happened to me and my response gives me the ability to discuss Depression, Despondency and How to be an Overcomer because I have battled and some days still battle Depression and Despondency. However, by taking myself to prayer when I don't feel it and listening to God I am learning to be a Victor and not a victim.

Below is the list in order:

1) My deceased husband's brush with possible colon cancer;
2) A major surgery and two weeks in the hospital for him;
3) I became septic having emergency gallbladder surgery;
4) 2008 diagnosed with pancreatic cancer;
5) Many surgeries, almost two years of hospital stays and a few near death experiences;
6) Finding out my husband was taking my prescription dilaudid out of my IV bags and putting water in them because he was in pain and addicted to prescription drugs, then beginning the process to get him help;
7) Hearing the love of my life fire a gun in the wall to scare us wanting us to think he had committed suicide,
8) Subsequently, having him arrested, appearing before a judge with him in shackles,
9) Three stays in drug rehabilitation and one stay in detox for him.
10) Taking a position as #2 in a small company, consequently being fired for supposed inadequate leadership skills while income and employee morale increased as payables decreased.
11) A rock hitting my oil pan causing two weeks without a car while a specialty dealer replaced the oil pan for $1,100.
12) Extreme pain from bad teeth
13) Being told I could have possible lung cancer

14) On the evangelism field in Houston my car springing a leak in the radiator. No money with repair costs of over $1,200
15) My husband dying from a prescription drug overdose.
16) I was forced to have his body cremated because of a family situation.
17) I was interrogated by the State Police for his possible murder until they ruled it an accidental suicide.
18) Homeowners insurance being cancelled; having a yard sale selling everything I could to come up with the money to pay the policy after convincing them to issue it in my name since the deed had not been changed yet.
19) Attacked verbally by a friend of my son's and her mother regarding our family situation;
20) My son unexpectedly moving out and in with a friend's family.
21) Both of our vehicles breaking down within two weeks of each other.
22) The refrigerator quit working in the middle of winter. No money to buy a new one. Using a cooler on the porch.
23) Christmas alone,
24) The commode messed up forcing me to learn how to turn the water off.
25) The water pipes freezing and bursting (thank God for homeowners insurance). I learned with help from friends how to replace pipes and tear out sheetrock.
26) Bishop James L. Kilgore dying unexpectedly - 2nd most influential man in my life other than my husband and father.
27) My dad becoming ill, spending three days with him in the hospital.
28) I had a heart attack.
29) Becoming extremely ill my last day in Africa.
30) My Dad dying while I was on a plane coming home from Africa.

31) I was mentally and physically incapable of attending my father's funeral.
32) Falling into a baptistry before ministering to over 600 ladies at a ladies conference.
33) Verbally being attacked by friends who are like family(jealousy is a horrible disease)
34) Staying subsequently with a someone who had challenges.
35) Keys to my car disappearing having to call a locksmith.
36) Someone trying to do everything to destroy me and God's ministry He has allowed me to be a small part of.

The secret to continuing no matter what is to remain still standing... Still praying.... You have to still keep putting God first regardless. Yes, I have made missteps and mistakes but I know how to go to my knees in prayer.

You can wear your depression like a blanket or wave it like a trophy. In my mind both are wrong and inconsistent with a Christian lifestyle. Depression is not a sin but letting it continue I think is a sin. You have to seek help on your knees, in your Bible, with your pastor and with professional counselors who can help you.

You may not want anyone to know you are battling this but you are. You have to grow up and ask for help. True mature Christians know when to ask for help. This will help you grow more in your walk with God. In order to lay the depression down you must learn how to be an overcomer.

God gave me many miracles throughout this process. However, I had to learn to respond to the problems correctly. That is what this book has been about. It is about how God taught me to respond.

Do I do it right all the time? Absolutely not but I try.

I know how to repent, do you?

Most have not learned the two most important secrets of success....

Repentance first and then Worship regardless of your situation or problem!

Worship through it!

Call on Jesus first when reeling from shock. In the beginning you just reel than you call on the name of the one who will rescue you.

If there is anything I hope you get from this book it is the following:

1. Prayer daily – many times a day.
   I Thessalonians 5:17, "Pray without ceasing."
2. Bible reading – daily – two to three times a day.
   It's not about quantity of scripture read but about quality.
3. Developing a relationship with Jesus that is like talking to your best friend and then listening for His response.
   JESUS WILL RESPOND!
4. Repent for not being willing to forgive those that have wronged you. Repent for other sins you have done.
5. Forgive – truly forgive whether others ask for it or not.
   Trust God to help you forgive
6. Worship God through every situation and circumstance.
7. Thank God for leading you and directing you.

I can only hope that how God has led me through the greatest battle of my life for my soul helps you one tenth of how it has helped me. We have to give God control of our lives even those parts that are dark and ugly like depression.

So, I think we all need to go pray and seek God's face.

Please know I am praying for you!

Other Books by Susan D. Smith

Surprised by God with Pancreatic Cancer

My Child, I've Got This

Living the Miracle

Falling Back Into The Arms of God...
Stripped & Broken

The Blood

COMING SOON

Just Tagging Along With Jesus, Adventures in
Kenya (Spring 2015)

Write it On the Doorposts of My Heart   (Spring
2015)

Two Destiny's One Outcome (Spring 2015)
Joyful in All Things (Spring 2015)
Adventures of the Yellow Convertible Bug (Winter
2015)

Cherry Blossoms (Spring 2015)

AVAILABLE

Susan D. Smith

To come to your church

Or

Civic organization

To build faith and hope

(304) 640-5717

Facebook: Susan D Wine Smith
Twitter: @Susanht9
Instagram: susanht9
Email: susanht9@gmail.com

Made in the USA
Columbia, SC
11 June 2018